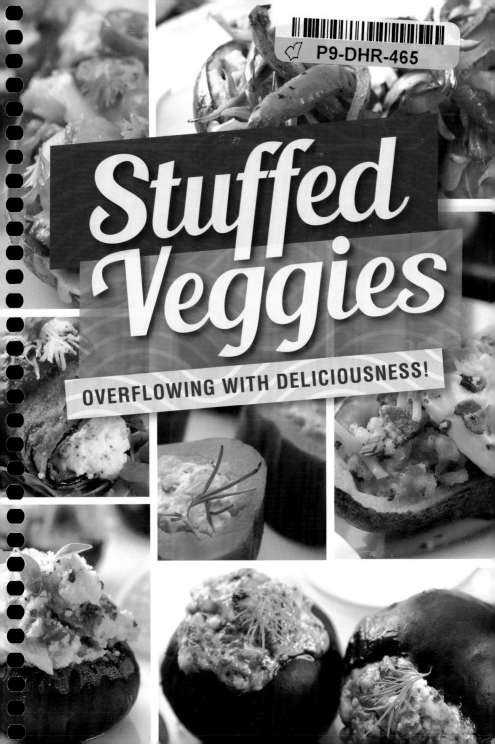

Stuffed Veggies

OVERFLOWING WITH DELICIOUSNESS!

Pick the best & bring 'em home

Artichokes. tightly packed, pointed green leaves with a purple or brownish tint

Avocados. dark-colored leathery skin that "gives" slightly when pressed gently

Beets. a uniformly round shape, 1½" to 2" in diameter; smooth unblemished skin with deep reddish-purple color; firm texture; bright green leaves

Cabbage. firm, crisp leaves in a compact head; small to medium size

Printed in the United States of America
by G&R Publishing Co.

Distributed By:

507 Industrial Street
Waverly, IA 50677

ISBN-13: 978-1-56383-537-7
Item #7123

Celery. crisp, glossy light to medium green stalks

Cucumbers. a straight even shape, firm texture, and a uniform green color

Eggplant. smooth, shiny skin that "gives" slightly when pressed gently; deep color; heavy for their size

Lettuce. crisp texture; bright color; fresh core

Mushrooms. clean and lightweight; firm texture; uniform color; plump stems

Onions. tight papery skin; dry, firm flesh

Peppers. shiny with bright color; firm skin

Potatoes & Sweet Potatoes. firm symmetrical shape; relatively smooth skin with only a few "eyes"

Squash *(Summer)*. bright glossy skin that "gives" slightly with gentle pressure

Squash *(Winter)*. heavy with intact stems

Tomatoes. rich colored skin that "gives" slightly when pressed gently

... now, let's get stuffin'!

Fajita-Filled Avocados

1 lb. flat iron or skirt steak

Salt & black pepper to taste

2½ T. dry fajita seasoning, divided

2½ T. fresh chopped cilantro

1 red bell pepper, sliced & seeded

2 jalapeños, sliced & seeded

1 onion, sliced

4 avocados

¼ C. lemon juice, divided

Arugula

Sprinkle the steak with salt, pepper, and 1 tablespoon fajita seasoning and place in a zippered plastic bag; toss in the cilantro. Zip it up and refrigerate for at least 1 hour to let those flavors really blend.

continued on next page...

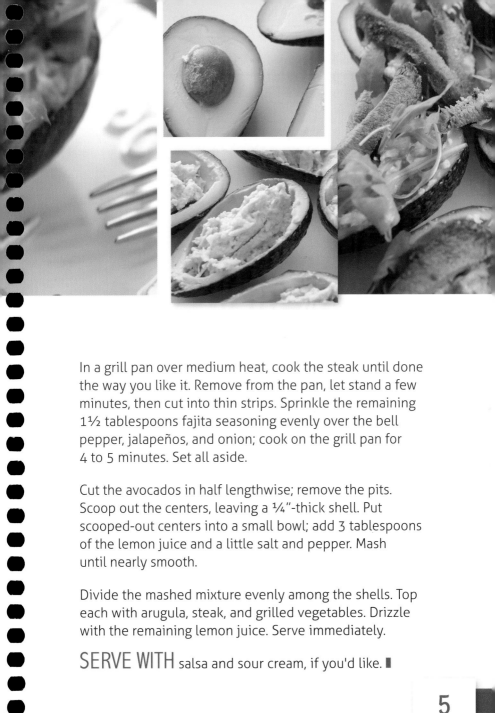

In a grill pan over medium heat, cook the steak until done the way you like it. Remove from the pan, let stand a few minutes, then cut into thin strips. Sprinkle the remaining 1½ tablespoons fajita seasoning evenly over the bell pepper, jalapeños, and onion; cook on the grill pan for 4 to 5 minutes. Set all aside.

Cut the avocados in half lengthwise; remove the pits. Scoop out the centers, leaving a ¼"-thick shell. Put scooped-out centers into a small bowl; add 3 tablespoons of the lemon juice and a little salt and pepper. Mash until nearly smooth.

Divide the mashed mixture evenly among the shells. Top each with arugula, steak, and grilled vegetables. Drizzle with the remaining lemon juice. Serve immediately.

SERVE WITH salsa and sour cream, if you'd like. ∎

Cajun Crab Mushrooms

Butter

2 (8 oz.) pkgs. baby portobello or white mushrooms

1 T. each finely chopped onion & red bell pepper

¾ C. refrigerated chunk-style crabmeat, coarsely chopped

2 T. finely chopped green onion

1 tsp. minced garlic

¼ tsp. Cajun seasoning

Salt & black pepper to taste

¼ C. plain Greek yogurt

1 T. half & half

½ C. bread crumbs

Hot sauce to taste

Juice from 1 lemon, divided

1 T. grated Parmesan cheese

Preheat the oven to 350°. Grease a shallow baking pan with 1 tablespoon butter. Remove and chop the mushroom stems. Brush the insides of the mushroom caps with melted butter and arrange them in the prepared pan, hollow side up. Set aside.

Pour 3 tablespoons melted butter into a small skillet. Add the mushroom stems, onion, and bell peppers; cook until tender, then transfer to a bowl. Stir in the crabmeat, green onion, garlic, Cajun seasoning, salt, pepper, yogurt, half & half, bread crumbs, hot sauce, and half the lemon juice; divide evenly among the mushroom caps and sprinkle with the cheese.

Bake for 15 to 20 minutes or until heated through.

DRIZZLE WITH the remaining lemon juice. ∎

Shredded Beef Mini Bell Nachos

1½ lbs. mini bell peppers, stems removed

1 T. olive oil

½ onion, diced

¾ tsp. minced garlic

3 C. shredded cooked beef

Salt & black pepper to taste

1 (4 oz.) can diced green chiles, drained

1 (2.25 oz.) can sliced black olives, drained

2 tomatoes, diced

1 C. shredded Pepper Jack cheese

2 C. shredded cheddar cheese

Preheat the oven to 350°. Slice the peppers in half lengthwise and remove the seeds; arrange peppers on a greased rimmed baking sheet, cut side up.

Heat the oil in a big skillet over medium heat. Add the onion and cook until softened. Then add the garlic and beef, stirring until heated through; sprinkle with salt and pepper.

Layer the beef mixture, chiles, olives, tomatoes, and both cheeses over the peppers.

Bake for 6 to 8 minutes or until the cheese is melted and everything is good and hot.

SERVE WITH sour cream and/or guacamole. ∎

Filled Popper
Potatoes

Olive oil

5 baking potatoes

1 onion, finely chopped

4 jalapeños, seeded & finely chopped

½ tsp. minced garlic

½ tsp. each salt & black pepper

1 C. shredded cheddar cheese

½ (4 oz.) container feta cheese

3 bacon strips, cooked & crumbled

3 green onions, thinly sliced

Melted butter

Preheat the oven to 375°. Rub oil over whole potatoes and cut a small slit in the top of each; arrange on a rimmed baking sheet and bake for 1 hour or until done. Set aside until cool enough to handle.

Meanwhile, heat 1 tablespoon oil in a big skillet. Add the onion and jalapeños; cook until softened, stirring occasionally. Add the garlic and cook for 1 minute longer. Transfer the mixture to a bowl and let cool slightly. Add the salt, pepper, and both cheeses; mash, then stir in the bacon and green onions.

Cut potatoes in half lengthwise and scoop out the centers, leaving a ¼"- to ½"-thick shell. Add the scooped-out centers to the bowl with the cheese mixture and mash until blended. Brush the shells inside and out with melted butter. Fill the shells with the cheese mixture and arrange them on the baking sheet.

Bake for 10 minutes or until heated through.

SERVE WITH sour cream, chives, bacon, and cheddar cheese. ∎

Portobello "Pasta" Bowls

1 small spaghetti squash

Olive oil

Salt, black pepper, garlic powder & onion powder to taste

1 T. grated Parmesan cheese

1 T. melted butter

2 large portobello mushroom caps

½ to 1 C. of your favorite pasta sauce

¼ to ½ C. finely shredded Italian cheese blend

Italian seasoning or dried basil to taste

Preheat the oven to 425°. Line a rimmed baking sheet with parchment paper. Carefully cut the squash in half lengthwise and remove the seeds. Drizzle oil over the flesh, sprinkle with salt and pepper, and place cut side down on the prepared baking sheet. Bake 1 hour or until tender; set aside until cool enough to handle. Don't turn off the oven.

Scrape the squash with a fork to remove flesh in long strands. Measure 1 cup of strands into a bowl; stir in garlic powder, onion powder, Parmesan cheese, and butter. You won't use the remaining squash for this recipe.

Remove the stem and gills from the underside of each mushroom cap by scraping with a spoon. Place the caps in a parchment paper-lined baking pan, hollow side up. Layer half the squash, pasta sauce, and cheese blend in each cap; sprinkle with Italian seasoning.

Bake for 10 minutes or until the cheese melts and the mushrooms have softened. ∎

SERVES 6

Feta Cucumber Cups

2 cucumbers, ends
  trimmed

1 (4 oz.) container
  crumbled feta cheese

¼ C. plain Greek yogurt

1 tsp. dried oregano

1 tsp. lemon juice, optional

Black pepper & red pepper
  flakes to taste

2 T. each chopped
  kalamata olives, sundried
  tomatoes & roasted red
  peppers, drained

Cut cucumbers into ¾"-thick slices. Using a melon baller,
dig out the middle of each slice, without cutting through
the bottom; blot dry. In a bowl, mash the cheese with the
yogurt; stir in the oregano, lemon juice, black pepper, red
pepper flakes, olives, sundried tomatoes, and peppers.
Divide the mixture evenly among the cucumber cups. ▌

Raw Zucchini Sushi Rolls

¼ C. raw cashews, soaked
   in water overnight

1½ tsp. rice vinegar

½ avocado, pitted & peeled

Red pepper flakes, salt &
   black pepper to taste

2 zucchini, ends trimmed

1 carrot, sliced into
   matchsticks

½ seedless cucumber,
   sliced into matchsticks

2 radishes, sliced & halved

Fresh cilantro

Sesame seed

Drain the cashews; process with the vinegar and avocado
in a food processor until a soft chunky paste forms. Stir
in pepper flakes, salt, and pepper. Cut long thin strips
from the zucchini; blot dry. Put a spoonful of the cashew
mixture along the length of each zucchini strip. Roll
up some of the veggies and cilantro in each strip and
sprinkle with sesame seed and more pepper flakes. ∎

15

Summer Squash Taco Boats

¼ C. thick salsa

4 yellow summer squash

Salt

1 T. vegetable oil

1 lb. ground turkey or beef

1 tsp. each garlic powder, ground cumin, chili powder & paprika

½ tsp. ground oregano

½ onion, finely chopped

2 T. finely chopped red and/or green bell pepper

½ C. taco sauce

½ C. shredded Mexican cheese blend

Preheat the oven to 400°. Spread ¼ C. salsa on the bottom of a greased 9 x 13" baking dish; set aside.

Cut squash in half lengthwise and remove seeds. Using a melon baller or spoon, remove some of the center, leaving a ¼"-thick shell. Chop the removed squash and roll it up in a paper towel to squeeze out excess liquid. Meanwhile, bring a big saucepan of water to a boil; add 1 tablespoon salt and the squash shells; boil for 1 minute. Transfer shells to paper towels, hollow side down. Set all aside.

Heat the oil in a big skillet over medium heat. Add the turkey and cook until no longer pink, breaking it apart while it cooks; drain. Stir in the garlic powder, cumin, 1 teaspoon salt, chili powder, paprika, oregano, onion, bell pepper, taco sauce, chopped squash, and ¼ cup water. Reduce heat to low, cover, and simmer for 20 minutes. Spoon the mixture into the shells, top with cheese, and set into the prepared dish; cover. Bake for 35 minutes or until tender. ∎

Asian Pork & Mushroom Cabbage Rolls

1 lg. head Napa cabbage

2 T. canola oil

1 tsp. sesame oil

2 tsp. ground ginger

3 garlic cloves, finely chopped

4 oz. shiitake mushrooms, thinly sliced

1 lb. ground pork

1 C. cooked long-grain white rice

1 carrot, shredded

3 green onions, sliced

¼ C. chopped fresh cilantro

Pinch of red pepper flakes

1 T. soy sauce

1 T. rice wine vinegar

¼ C. plus 2 T. hoisin sauce, divided

continued on next page...

Preheat the oven to 375°. Carefully remove the leaves from the cabbage and cut about 2" off the end of the hard core; dip each leaf briefly in boiling water and set aside on paper towels.

Heat both oils together in a medium skillet. Add the ginger, garlic, and mushrooms; cook for 5 minutes.

In a big bowl, stir together the pork, rice, carrot, green onions, cilantro, red pepper flakes, soy sauce, vinegar, and ¼ cup hoisin sauce until well mixed. Stir in the mushroom mixture.

Scoop ¼ to ½ cup of the rice mixture *(depending on the size of your leaves)* onto the stem end of each leaf and roll toward the leaf end, folding in the sides if you'd like. Place seam side down on a foil-lined, greased baking sheet.

Mix the remaining 2 tablespoons hoisin sauce and 1 tablespoon water; brush over the top and sides of each cabbage roll. Bake for 30 to 35 minutes or until the pork is done. ∎

Loaded Apple
Sweet Potatoes

2 small sweet potatoes

Olive oil

1 Golden Delicious apple, cored

¼ C. melted butter

2 T. applesauce

2 T. pure maple syrup

¼ C. finely chopped pecans

¼ C. chopped dried cranberries

½ tsp. cinnamon

A pinch of salt

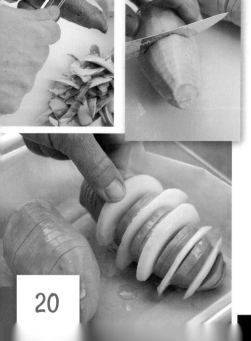

Preheat the oven to 400°. Line a small baking dish with parchment paper; set aside. Pierce the sweet potatoes a few times and microwave each one on high for 1½ minutes.

When cool enough to handle, peel the sweet potatoes and rub oil over the surface of each one. Cut ¼"-thick widthwise slices into the potatoes without cutting through the bottom. Set the potatoes in the prepared baking dish.

Cut the apple into very thin rings and cut the rings in half; dip into the melted butter and place one slice between alternate cuts in the sweet potatoes. Cover with foil and bake for 40 minutes.

Stir together the applesauce, syrup, pecans, cranberries, cinnamon, and salt. Remove the dish from the oven *(don't turn off the oven)* and carefully push some of the pecan mixture between the empty cuts in the sweet potatoes, putting any extra filling on top.

Bake uncovered 10 to 15 minutes, watching carefully so the pecan mixture doesn't burn.

SERVE WITH maple syrup, if you'd like. ∎

Sausage-Rice Onion Bowls

8 large onions, any kind, peeled

⅓ C. fresh bread crumbs

3½ tsp. olive oil, divided

Coarse salt & black pepper

½ lb. Italian sausage

½ each green & red bell pepper, chopped

½ tsp. minced garlic

¼ C. shredded Parmesan cheese

2 C. cooked long-grain white rice

Preheat the oven to 375°. Grease a 9 x 13" baking pan. In a large saucepan, bring ½" of water to a boil. Add onions, cover, and boil for 15 minutes, until slightly soft; remove with a slotted spoon. Stir together bread crumbs, ½ teaspoon oil, salt, and pepper. Set all aside.

When cool enough to handle, cut off the top ⅓ of each onion and dig out the center with a spoon, leaving only the two outer rings intact, without cutting through the bottom; cut off a small slice from the bottom so they set flat. Arrange in the prepared pan, hollow side up.

In a skillet, cook the sausage in 1 teaspoon hot oil until browned, breaking it apart while it cooks. Transfer to a bowl using a slotted spoon. Add 1 teaspoon oil to the grease in the skillet; when hot, add the peppers, garlic, salt and pepper. Cook for 8 minutes or until just tender; add to the sausage along with the cheese, rice, remaining 1 teaspoon oil, salt, and pepper. Stuff the mixture into the onions; top with the set-aside bread crumbs. Bake for 30 minutes or until tender. ▮

Philly Cheesesteak Stuffed Peppers

2 T. butter

2 T. olive oil

1 sweet onion, sliced

1 (8 oz.) pkg. baby portobello mushrooms, sliced

Salt & black pepper to taste

8 oz. thinly sliced deli roast beef

2 to 3 tsp. minced garlic

2 large green bell peppers, stems removed

8 slices provolone cheese

Heat the butter and oil in a big skillet over medium-low heat until butter melts. Add the onion, mushrooms, salt,

continued on next page...

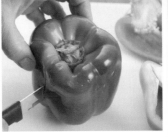

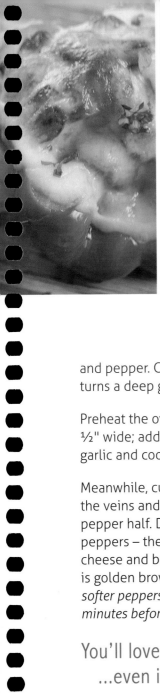

and pepper. Cook for 20 to 30 minutes or until everything turns a deep golden brown.

Preheat the oven to 400°. Cut the beef into strips about ½" wide; add them to the onion mixture along with the garlic and cook 5 minutes longer.

Meanwhile, cut the peppers in half lengthwise; remove the veins and seeds. Lay one slice of cheese inside each pepper half. Divide the onion mixture evenly among the peppers – they will be full! Top each with another slice of cheese and bake for 20 to 30 minutes or until the cheese is golden brown and the peppers are crisp-tender. *(For softer peppers, try steaming them in the oven for 5 to 10 minutes before adding the filling.)* ▌

You'll love these...
    ...even if you aren't from Philly!

Adobo Sweet Skins

3 medium sweet potatoes

1 lb. boneless chicken breast

Salt & black pepper to taste

1½ T. plus ¼ C. olive oil, divided

2 tsp. minced garlic

Juice of 1 lime

3 chipotle peppers in adobo, chopped

1 tsp. each dried oregano & cumin

2 tsp. chili powder

2 C. fresh baby spinach

4 oz. shredded Monterey Jack cheese

Preheat the oven to 375°. Prick the potatoes with a fork and bake 1 hour or until tender. Place the chicken in a separate baking dish, sprinkle with salt and pepper, and drizzle with 1 tablespoon of oil. Bake alongside the potatoes for the last 30 minutes, until done. Meanwhile, stir together garlic, lime juice, chipotle peppers, oregano, cumin, chili powder, 1 teaspoon salt, ½ teaspoon pepper, and ¼ cup oil. Set all aside for 15 minutes. Increase the oven temperature to 400°.

Cut each potato into four even wedges. Scoop out the centers, leaving a ¼"-thick shell. You won't use the removed sweet potato for this recipe. Brush the inside of each shell with some chipotle mixture and bake on a greased rimmed baking sheet for 10 minutes. Shred the chicken and stir it into the remaining chipotle mixture. Heat the remaining 1½ teaspoons oil in a skillet over medium heat. Add the spinach, stirring until it wilts; stir into the chicken mixture. Mound the mixture on the shells; top each with a little cheese. Bake 10 minutes longer or until the cheese melts. ∎

Inside-Out Pickle Rolls

5 whole dill pickles, ends trimmed

½ (8 oz.) pkg. cream cheese, softened

1 T. dry fiesta ranch dip mix

4-5 slices deli ham, finely chopped

Using a sharp knife and working from both ends, carefully cut a hole lengthwise through the center of each pickle. Set the pickles upright on paper towels to drain for 30 minutes.

Stir together the cream cheese, dressing mix, and ham. Transfer the mixture to a pastry bag fitted with a large round tip; pipe the mixture into the pickles. Wrap the filled pickles in plastic wrap and chill for 2 hours. Cut the pickles into 1" slices. ▌

Pesto Avocado Tomatoes

30 grape or cherry
   tomatoes

½ avocado

2 oz. cream cheese spread

1 T. basil pesto

½ tsp. lemon juice

Line a tray with paper towels. Cut a thin slice from the top of each tomato *(cut a thin slice from the bottom, too, if necessary, so they stand upright)*. With a small spoon, sharp knife, or the tip of a vegetable peeler, hollow out the tomatoes, leaving a thin shell *(don't cut through the bottom)*. Invert the tomatoes on the paper towels and let them drain for 30 minutes.

Combine avocado, cream cheese, pesto, and lemon juice; mash until smooth. Transfer the mixture to a pastry bag fitted with a large round tip; pipe the mixture into the tomato shells. ∎

Southwest Spaghetti
Squash

1 medium spaghetti squash

1 T. olive oil

½ red onion, chopped

1 jalapeño pepper, finely chopped

1 red bell pepper, chopped

2 chipotle peppers in adobo, chopped

1 tsp. minced garlic

1½ tsp. each ground cumin, dried oregano & chili powder

Coarse salt & black pepper to taste

1 (15 oz.) can black beans, drained & rinsed

1 C. frozen corn, thawed

Juice & zest of 1 lime

½ C. chopped fresh cilantro, divided

½ C. each shredded cheddar & Monterey Jack cheese

Preheat the oven to 375°. Pierce the shell of the squash several times with a sharp knife and set on a rimmed baking sheet. Bake for 1 hour or until tender. Let set until cool enough to handle.

Meanwhile, heat oil in a skillet over medium heat. Add the onion, jalapeño, bell pepper, and chipotle peppers; cook for 2 minutes. Add the garlic, cumin, oregano, chili powder, salt and pepper; cook for another minute. Stir in the beans, corn, lime juice, and half the cilantro.

Cut the squash in half lengthwise and remove the seeds. Gently scrape the inside with a fork to remove it in long spaghetti-like strands; add the strands to the mixture in the skillet and stir in the cheese. Mound the mixture evenly into the squash halves and sprinkle with the lime zest and remaining cilantro. Serve immediately. ∎

What looks like pasta, but isn't? Delicious, nutritious spaghetti squash!

MAKES 8

Oktoberfest Potato Skins

Vegetable oil

Salt & coarse black pepper to taste

4 russet potatoes

2 bratwursts, cut into small pieces

2 onions, thinly sliced

½ C. Oktoberfest-type beer

2 T. melted butter

½ C. each shredded Gruyère & white cheddar cheese

½ C. drained sauerkraut

Preheat the oven to 400°. Line a big baking sheet with foil; set aside.

Stir together 2 tablespoons oil, salt, and pepper; rub over the surface of the potatoes. Arrange the potatoes on the baking sheet and bake for 1 hour or until tender. Set aside until cool enough to handle.

continued on next page...

Meanwhile, heat a little oil in a skillet and add the bratwurst pieces, cooking until brown on all sides and no longer pink in the middle; transfer to paper towels to drain. Pour a little oil in the skillet; add the onions, salt, and pepper and cook over medium-low heat for 20 to 30 minutes or until deep golden brown. Add the drained bratwurst pieces and the beer; cook until slightly thickened.

Cut the potatoes in half lengthwise and scoop out the centers, leaving a ¼"-thick shell. You won't use the removed potato for this recipe. Return the shells to the baking sheet. Brush melted butter inside each shell and season with salt and pepper. Turn oven to broil and broil the potatoes for a few minutes until slightly brown. Flip the potatoes over and broil a few minutes longer, until slightly crisp. Divide the bratwurst mixture and both cheeses evenly among the shells. Broil a few seconds to melt the cheese. Top with sauerkraut and a little pepper. ▮

Stuffed Zucchini Shells

2 zucchini

3 bacon strips, cooked & crumbled

2 T. butter

1 C. chopped onion

¼ tsp. curry powder

1 T. sour cream

¾ tsp. dried thyme

1½ tsp. salt, divided

¼ tsp. coarse black pepper

½ tomato, chopped

Shredded Gouda cheese

Preheat the oven to 400°. Slice the zucchini in half lengthwise and use a spoon to scoop out the pulp, leaving a ½"-thick shell. Set the zucchini halves in a greased baking pan. Chop the pulp and toss it in a bowl with the bacon; set aside.

Melt the butter in a skillet; add the onion and cook until tender. Stir in the curry powder, cook 30 seconds more, and transfer the mixture to the bowl with the zucchini and bacon. Stir in the sour cream, thyme, salt, pepper, and tomato. Divide the mixture evenly among the zucchini halves; sprinkle each with a little cheese.

Bake for 20 minutes. Turn on the broiler and broil for 2 to 3 minutes or until the tops are golden brown. ∎

Crabby Romaine

1 (8 oz.) pkg. refrigerated
  chunk-style crabmeat,
  coarsely chopped

2 T. each mayonnaise
  & plain yogurt

2 to 3 tsp. Sriracha sauce

1 T. rice vinegar

Salt & coarse black pepper
  to taste

1 head Romaine lettuce

Avocado and/or cucumber

Fresh dill

Stir together the crabmeat, mayonnaise, yogurt, Sriracha sauce, vinegar, salt, and pepper.

Remove the outer leaves from the head of Romaine; you won't use them for this recipe. Carefully remove some of the smaller leaves and fill each of them with crab mixture.

Just before you serve these beauties, dice up some avocado and/or cucumber and lay the pieces on top of each filled leaf. Sprinkle with some extra pepper and a little dill. ▌

These make an excellent side salad, light lunch, or hefty appetizer.

Eggplant Parmesan Rolls

1 (15 oz.) container ricotta cheese

½ C. grated Romano cheese

1½ T. minced garlic

2 tsp. Italian seasoning

Salt & coarse black pepper to taste

3 eggs

1 C. flour

1 C. dried seasoned bread crumbs

Vegetable oil for frying

1 large eggplant, stem removed

Preheat the oven to 400°. Grease a 9 x 13" baking pan and set aside. In a mixing bowl, beat the ricotta and Romano cheeses, garlic, Italian seasoning, salt, and pepper on medium speed until smooth and creamy. Chill until needed.

continued on next page...

Place the eggs in a shallow bowl and beat them well. Put the flour and bread crumbs in separate shallow bowls.

Heat several inches of oil in a large saucepan or deep-fryer to 375°. While the oil heats, cut the eggplant into ¼"-thick lengthwise slices, discarding the tiny end pieces. Dredge both sides of one or two eggplant slices in flour, shaking off any excess. Submerge the flour-coated slices in the egg and then dredge both sides in bread crumbs. Slowly lower the coated slices into the hot oil. Fry until light golden brown, turning occasionally. Remove and drain on paper towels and repeat with the remaining slices. Chill the fried slices for 10 minutes.

Generously mound some of the chilled cheese mixture on the center of each chilled eggplant slice and roll up from a short end. Place rolls in the prepared baking pan, seam side down. Bake for 20 to 25 minutes or until heated through.

SERVE WITH your favorite pasta sauce. ∎

Nice and thin
makes for
easy rolling.

Hot Tuna
Tomato Shells

4 large tomatoes

2 (5 oz.) cans water-packed tuna, drained & flaked

3 T. chopped onion

½ C. shredded cheddar cheese

¼ C. each mayonnaise & sour cream

¾ tsp. onion powder

½ tsp. coarse salt

⅛ tsp. coarse black pepper

½ tsp. dried dill weed

2 tsp. dill pickle relish

⅔ C. coarsely crushed potato chips, plus more for sprinkling

Preheat the oven to 350°. Coat a 9 x 9" baking dish with cooking spray. Cut off a thin slice from the top of each tomato; set the tops aside. Using a spoon, scoop out and discard the centers to create a shell.

Stir together the tuna, onion, cheese, mayonnaise, sour cream, onion powder, salt, pepper, dill weed, and pickle relish until well blended; gently stir in the ⅔ cup crushed potato chips. Stuff the mixture evenly into the tomato shells, mounding the top; arrange them in the prepared baking dish.

Pop the tops back onto the tomatoes, cover everything with foil, and bake for 20 minutes.

Remove the foil and discard the tomato tops; add some extra crushed potato chips and bake for 10 to 15 minutes longer or until the filling is hot and the chips are toasted.

GARNISH WITH a little paprika and fresh dill. ∎

Way better than Mama's tuna casserole — but don't tell her!

Popeye's Artichoke Hearts

1 (14.5 oz.) can whole
artichoke hearts, drained

1 (10 oz.) box frozen
chopped spinach,
thawed

1 T. vegetable oil

¼ C. finely chopped onion

1 T. minced garlic

2 T. Parmesan cheese

½ tsp. salt

¼ tsp. black pepper

Shredded mozzarella
cheese

Preheat the broiler and coat a broiler pan with cooking
spray. Slice each artichoke heart in half lengthwise. Pull
out the centers of each half and turn the halves upside-
down on paper towels; chop the pulled-out centers.
Drain the spinach and squeeze out as much moisture as
possible. Set all aside.

continued on next page...

If you have any extra filling, just heat it up; it tastes great on crackers, too.

In a skillet, heat the oil over medium heat. Add the onion and cook until tender. Toss in the spinach, breaking it apart into strands. Add the garlic, Parmesan cheese, salt, pepper, and set-aside chopped artichoke; heat until everything is warm.

Divide the spinach mixture among the artichoke hearts, mounding it on top. Add a bit of mozzarella cheese to each.

Broil 4" from the heat for a few minutes, until the cheese melts and turns a deep golden brown. ∎

Spaghetti Squash Lasagna

2 large spaghetti squash

Olive oil

Salt & black pepper to taste

1 onion, chopped

2 tsp. minced garlic

1¼ lbs. each ground pork & pork sausage

1 (16 oz.) can petite diced tomatoes

2 tsp. each dried oregano, Italian seasoning & red pepper flakes, divided

½ C. each ricotta cheese & cottage cheese

1 C. shredded mozzarella cheese

Preheat the oven to 400°. Carefully slice each squash in half lengthwise and remove the seeds. Rub oil over the cut edges and inside each half; season with salt and pepper. Arrange on a rimmed baking sheet, cut side down; bake for 1 hour or until just tender.

Meanwhile, heat 1 tablespoon oil in a big saucepan over medium heat. Add the onion, garlic, all the meat, and some salt and pepper. Cook until the meat is no longer pink, breaking it apart while it cooks; drain. Stir in the tomatoes and 1 teaspoon each oregano, Italian seasoning, and red pepper flakes. Bring the mixture to a boil; reduce the heat to low and simmer a few minutes to thicken. Mix the ricotta cheese, cottage cheese, the remaining 1 teaspoon each oregano, Italian seasoning, and red pepper flakes, and a little more salt and pepper.

Reduce the oven temperature to 350°. Scrape the inside of the squash with a fork; pile the ricotta mixture, meat mixture, and mozzarella cheese on top. Bake 30 minutes, until heated through. ▪

Kale & Bacon Breakfast Bells

2 bell peppers, any color

3 bacon strips

½ sweet onion, diced

½ tomato, seeded & chopped

1 C. chopped fresh kale

3 eggs

2 T. milk

Salt, black pepper & garlic powder to taste

½ C. shredded provolone cheese

Preheat the oven to 350°. Cut the peppers in half lengthwise; remove seeds and veins. Arrange the peppers in a greased 9 x 13" baking pan.

continued on next page...

Cook the bacon in a skillet until it's nice and crisp; remove the bacon and drain on paper towels, but leave the grease in the pan. Add the onion to the skillet and cook for 3 minutes. Stir in the tomato and kale. Crumble the bacon and return to the pan; cook 3 minutes longer or until the kale is wilted. Divide the mixture evenly among the pepper halves.

Whisk the eggs and milk together until well blended; pour slowly and evenly over the vegetable mixture in the peppers.

Bake for 30 to 35 minutes or until the eggs are nearly set. Then top each pepper with some of the cheese and bake 5 minutes longer or until the cheese is melted. ▌

You can use green bells, too, which aren't as sweet as the yellow, orange, or red ones.

Fiesta Ranch Jalapeños

3 oz. cream cheese, softened

1 T. dry fiesta ranch dip mix

¼ C. finely shredded cheddar cheese

3 T. frozen pork sausage & bacon crumbles *(like Jimmy Dean brand)*

5 fresh jalapeño peppers

Coarse black pepper

Preheat the oven to 400°. Line a baking sheet with foil and set a baking rack over the top. Mix together the cream cheese, dip mix, cheddar cheese, and frozen crumbles. Cut the jalapeños in half lengthwise, scoop out the seeds and veins, and arrange the peppers on the rack. Divide the cream cheese mixture evenly among the pepper halves. Sprinkle with black pepper. Bake for 15 minutes or until the filling is hot. ∎

Eggs in Roasted Tomatoes

6 medium tomatoes

Olive oil

Salt & black pepper to taste

Garlic powder, celery flakes, and dried thyme to taste

6 eggs

Preheat the oven to 400°. Slice the top ⅓ off the tomatoes and scoop out the seeds; turn upside-down on paper towels to drain briefly.

Arrange the tomatoes in a muffin pan and drizzle with a bit of oil; sprinkle with salt, pepper, garlic powder, celery flakes, and thyme. Bake about 20 minutes or until just tender. Don't turn off the oven. Crack an egg into each tomato and bake for 15 minutes or until they're cooked the way you like them. Sprinkle with a little more salt and pepper. ∎

Stuffed Mashed Potatoes

1 egg, beaten

1 C. fresh bread crumbs or panko bread crumbs

Cayenne pepper to taste

5 potatoes

2 tsp. salt

1 tsp. black pepper

¾ C. shredded cheddar cheese

Vegetable oil

1 (8 oz.) pkg. fresh mushrooms *(any kind)*, diced

¾ lb. chicken breast, diced

½ C. sliced green onion

1½ to 2 tsp. garam masala or seasoning of your choice

½ C. diced roasted bell peppers, drained

Preheat the oven to 425°. Line a metal rimmed baking sheet with foil and coat foil with cooking spray. Put egg and breadcrumbs in separate shallow bowls. Stir cayenne pepper into the bread crumbs. Set all aside.

Cook the potatoes in boiling water until tender. Drain and set aside until cool enough to handle. Then peel and mash, adding the salt and pepper. Set aside until nearly cool, then stir in the cheese.

Meanwhile, heat a little oil in a skillet. Add the mushrooms, chicken, and green onions; sprinkle with garam masala and cook until the chicken is done. Stir in the diced peppers.

Scoop up a couple of tablespoons of the mashed potato mixture and flatten into a 4" to 5" circle, about ½" thick. Using a slotted spoon, place a heaping tablespoon of the chicken mixture into the center of each circle and fold the potato over, enclosing the filling inside; shape each into a ball. Roll the balls first in set-aside egg and then bread crumbs; arrange them on the prepared baking sheet.

Bake for 30 to 35 minutes or until nice and brown.

SERVE WITH bell pepper relish and sour cream. ∎

Blue Cheese Beets

4 medium beets

2 T. chopped walnuts

4 T. Gorgonzola, goat
   cheese, or cream cheese

½ tsp. minced garlic

Salt & black pepper
   to taste

Cut away all but an inch of the beet stems. Fill a saucepan with water and bring to a boil. Add beets and cook for 30 to 40 minutes or until just tender *(don't poke too many holes in them because the color will bleed)*.

Meanwhile, toast the walnuts by placing them in a single layer in a dry skillet over medium heat for 10 minutes or until golden brown, stirring occasionally. Transfer to a small bowl and let cool.

continued on next page...

Remove the beets from the boiling water and plunge them briefly into a bowl of ice water to stop the cooking. When cool enough to handle, peel the beets, cut off the stem, and cut a small slice from the bottom so they set flat. Using a small spoon or sharp knife, scoop out the center, leaving a ¼"-thick shell; set aside.

Preheat the broiler. Add the cheese, garlic, salt, and pepper to the bowl with the walnuts; stir to blend. Stuff the cheese mixture into the beets and arrange on a small rimmed baking sheet. Broil for a minute or two, until the cheese mixture is golden brown.

SERVE WITH blue cheese or ranch dressing on the side. ∎

Breakfast Sweet Potatoes

4 sweet potatoes

6 brown 'n' serve sausage links, sliced

5 eggs

Salt, black pepper, & red pepper flakes to taste

Shredded cheddar cheese

Mini bell pepper slices

Preheat the oven to 400°. Line a rimmed baking sheet with foil and coat the foil with cooking spray. Pierce each sweet potato several times with a fork and place on the prepared baking sheet. Bake for 45 to 60 minutes or until tender. Do not turn off the oven.

When they're cool enough to handle, cut the sweet potatoes in half lengthwise and scoop out the inside, leaving a ¼"- to ½"-thick shell. Set the shells on the baking sheet, cut side up. You won't use the removed sweet potato for this recipe.

Put the sausages and a little water in a skillet over medium heat. Whisk together the eggs, salt, pepper, and red pepper flakes until well mixed and pour them into the skillet with the sausages. Cook until the eggs are done, stirring occasionally.

Stuff the egg mixture into the sweet potato shells, sprinkle with cheese, and bake for 5 minutes or until the cheese is melted. Top with pepper slices.

SERVE WITH maple syrup. ▮

Quick Celery Bites

1 (8 oz.) pkg. cream cheese, softened

2 T. sour cream

¼ C. chopped walnuts

20 green olives with pimento, chopped

1 bunch celery

In a mixing bowl, beat together cream cheese and sour cream; stir in walnuts and olives.

Cut celery into bite-size pieces and stuff the cream cheese mixture into the celery. ▮

Salmon Salad Avocados

1 (7.5 oz.) can salmon, drained & flaked

2 T. each plain yogurt & mayonnaise

2 T. chopped dill pickle

1 T. chopped onion

½ tsp. dill weed

⅛ tsp. each garlic salt & coarse black pepper

3 avocados

Lemon juice

Combine the salmon, yogurt, mayonnaise, pickle, onion, dill weed, garlic salt, and pepper; blend well.

Cut the avocados in half lengthwise and remove the pits. Brush lemon juice over the flesh of the avocados and fill the cavity with the salmon mixture, packing gently. Drizzle with a little more lemon juice, if you'd like. Serve immediately. ∎

Garden Salad Cabbage Bowls

1 large purple cabbage

⅓ C. olive oil

2 T. lemon juice

1 T. lime juice

2 tsp. Dijon mustard

2 tsp. grated Romano cheese

Salt & black pepper to taste

1¼ C. cooked quinoa, chilled

1 C. frozen peas, thawed

4 radishes, sliced

1 large carrot, shredded

2 T. chopped red onion

Arugula

Remove two large outer leaves from the cabbage and set aside. You won't use the remaining cabbage for this recipe.

To make the dressing, whisk together the oil, lemon and lime juices, mustard, cheese, salt, and pepper. Refrigerate until ready to use.

Combine the quinoa, peas, radishes, carrot, onion, and a big handful of arugula. Divide this mixture among the cabbage leaves and drizzle with the chilled dressing. ∎

Grab a fork — it's time to eat!

Artichokes with Bacon
& Cheese

1 T. olive oil

½ C. finely chopped onion

2 tsp. minced garlic

1 tsp. dried thyme

½ tsp. dried fennel seed, crushed

1 C. fresh bread crumbs

1 bacon strip, cooked & finely chopped

2 T. grated Parmesan cheese

1 T. capers, drained

Salt & black pepper to taste

2 fresh artichokes, stems removed

1 lemon, halved

Chicken broth or white wine

Preheat the oven to 400°. In a skillet, heat the oil over medium heat. Add the onion and garlic; cook until softened. Stir in the thyme, fennel seed, bread crumbs, and bacon; cook until the bread crumbs begin to brown, stirring often. Remove from the heat; stir in the cheese and capers. Season with salt and pepper and set aside.

Pull off the outer layer of artichoke leaves and discard; slice off 1" from the top of the artichokes. With scissors, snip off the sharp tips of the outer leaves and rub all the cut edges with lemon. Pull out the soft leaves from the center of the artichoke and use a melon baller or a spoon to scoop out the prickly middle; discard. Squeeze a little lemon juice into the center of the artichoke.

Dividing the bread crumb mixture among the two artichokes, put some filling between each of the leaves, and then fill the center with the remainder. Set the filled artichokes upright in a small baking dish; pour broth into dish to a depth of 1". Cover with foil; bake for 1 hour or until tender and toasty. ▌

Pull off one leaf at a time *(get the filling, too)*; scrape the fleshy part at the base between your teeth. Discard the rest of the leaf.

SERVES 4

Hot-Sweet Acorn Rings

2 acorn squash

1 egg

2 T. milk

1 lb. ground Italian sausage

Onion salt to taste

1 C. chopped fresh baby spinach

1½ C. fresh bread crumbs

½ C. dried cranberries

1 T. each olive oil & maple syrup

Preheat the oven to 400°. Cut off a thin slice from both ends of each squash. Slice each squash into rings, about ¾" thick; remove seeds and divide the rings evenly in microwave-safe pans, arranging them in a single layer. Cover the pans with microwave-safe plastic wrap, leaving

continued on next page...

one corner uncovered. Microwave each pan on high for 3 minutes, then transfer the rings to a parchment paper-lined rimmed baking sheet.

Whisk together the egg and milk until well blended; set aside.

In a skillet, cook the sausage until no longer pink, breaking it apart while it cooks; drain off excess grease and sprinkle onion salt over the meat. Stir in the spinach, bread crumbs, dried cranberries, and set-aside egg mixture until well mixed.

Place equal amounts of the sausage mixture into the center of each squash ring, packing lightly. Mix together the oil and syrup and drizzle evenly over the rings and filling. Bake for 30 minutes or until squash is tender.

SERVE WITH maple syrup. ∎

Use a sharp knife to cut squash... and watch those fingers!

Index